D1627447

CHALLENGING MINDS. INSPIRING SUCCESS.

CITY COLLEGE
NORWICH

Please return on or before the last
date stamped below.
Contact: 01603 773 114 or
01603 773 224

2 0 OCT 2010

– 4 MAR 2014

A FINE WILL BE CHARGED FOR OVERDUE ITEMS

A WORLD OF RECIPES

The Caribbean

REVISED AND UPDATED

Julie McCulloch

Heinemann
LIBRARY

www.heinemannlibrary.co.uk
Visit our website to find out more
information about Heinemann
Library books.

To order:
☎ Phone +44 (0) 1865 888066
🖹 Fax +44 (0) 1865 314091
💻 Visit www.heinemannlibrary.co.uk

Edited by David Andrews and Diyan Leake
Designed by Richard Parker
Illustrated by Nicholas Beresford-Davis
Picture research by Mica Brancic
Originated by Chroma Graphics (Overseas) Pte Ltd
Printed and bound in China by Leo Paper Products Ltd

ISBN 978 0 431 11817 8 (hardback)
13 12 11 10 09
10 9 8 7 6 5 4 3 2 1

ISBN 978 0 431 11829 1 (paperback)
13 12 11 10 09
10 9 8 7 6 5 4 3 2 1

British Library Cataloguing in Publication Data
McCulloch, Julie, 1973-
   The Caribbean. - 2nd ed. - (A world of recipes)
A full catalogue record for this book is available from the
British Library.

Acknowledgments
We would like to thank the following for permission to
reproduce photographs: © Capstone Global Library Ltd/MM
Studios pp. **24**, **25**; © Corbis p. **7** (© Danny Lehman); Gareth
Boden pp. **8–23**, **26–43**; Getty Images p. **5** (Stone/© Jeff
Hunter); © Photolibrary Group p. **6** (Fresh Food Images/
© Martin Brigdale).

Cover photograph of black beans with plantains on rice
reproduced with permission of Getty Images (StockFood
Creative/Quentin Bacon).

Every effort has been made to contact copyright holders of
material reproduced in this book. Any omissions will be
rectified in subsequent printings if notice is given to the
publisher.

All the Internet addresses (URLs) given in this book were valid
at the time of going to press. However, due to the dynamic
nature of the Internet, some addresses may have changed, or
sites may have changed or ceased to exist since publication.
While the author and publisher regret any inconvenience this
may cause readers, no responsibility for any such changes can
be accepted by either the author or the publisher.

Contents

Key: *easy **medium ***difficult

Some words are shown in bold, **like this**. You can find out what they mean by looking in the glossary.

The Caribbean

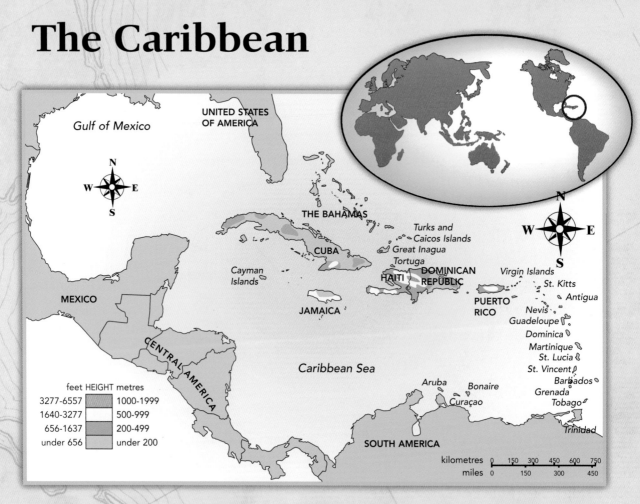

Surf, sand, and fresh seafood make the tropical islands of the Caribbean an appealing place to live in or visit. The islands stretch for over 4,000 kilometres (2,500 miles) off the coast of North and Central America.

Coral islands, such as the Bahamas, have beaches of white sand. Islands that sprang from volcanoes, such as Dominica, have beaches of black sand. There are several active volcanoes in the Caribbean.

The climate is hot and humid. Winds from the north-east bring moisture from the Atlantic Ocean. Many islands are green and fertile, though some are dry and desert-like. Hurricanes bring high winds between June and November.

In the past

The islands were first settled by people about 7,000 years ago. The first European to reach the islands was Christopher Columbus.

When Columbus came from Spain in 1492, three main groups of Indian people lived in the islands: the Arawaks, the Caribs, and the Ciboney. These islanders fished for seafood. Their crops included cassava, sweet potatoes, and maize. They ate wild fruit.

The Spanish arrived looking for gold. Soon, other countries, including Holland, France, and England, sent explorers to the islands. Wars were fought between the countries. Each country wanted to own the islands. Many pirates hid amongst the islands, especially around Tortuga.

Gradually, Europeans from different countries settled on different islands. The culture on the different islands were influenced in different ways. The Europeans grew sugar cane on plantations and brought slaves from Africa to work on them. The sugar was shipped to Europe for sale. The slaves also brought their own cultures to the islands. Near the end of the 19th century, slavery became illegal.

The Caribbean today

Almost all the islands are independent countries now. Islanders are descended from African slaves and from European settlers. They speak mainly English but also Spanish and French. They grow crops, fish, and provide services for tourists.

Tourists enjoy the resorts and beaches, dive to the coral reefs, and sail on boats. Carnivals are celebrated with costumes, parades, and dancing. Many festivals share music special to the islands, such as reggae and calypso.

↑ Tourists come to the Caribbean to dive among the tropical fish.

Caribbean food

The Caribs and Arawaks built grills of green sticks, called *barbacot*, over fires. Spanish settlers called this way of cooking *barbacoa*. In English we call it barbecue. Native ingredients are still used, including yams, taro roots, cassava, and beans.

The Europeans brought crops including oranges, coconuts, rice, and coffee. Slaves brought African food, including okra, pigeon peas, taro, breadfruit, and ackee, which are all different parts of plants that are used as vegetables.

Around the islands

Each island has a different style of cooking. It might be a blend of the native tradition on an island together with Spanish, African, French, or British ways of cooking.

In islands with English traditions, curried chicken and mutton (sheep meat) are eaten. In islands with French traditions, a stew uses goat meat, tomatoes, and papaya. Callaloo is from an African tradition. It is a soup using okra. Other African dishes include slow-cooked pigs' feet and cow heel soup.

↑ Seafood such as this crab dish is popular in the Caribbean.

Seafood is popular but it also varies between the islands. Flying fish is commonly eaten in Barbados. Trinidad and Tobago specialize in crab.

On islands such as Jamaica, the tropical climate allows fruit such as coconuts and bananas to grow. Sugar cane grows on volcanic islands such as St Kitts.

Caribbean meals

Traditional meals have three courses. The starter might be fruit or vegetables, either in a soup or fried. The main course is often meat served with rice. Each island serves slightly different rice with peas, beans, or coconut. The final course at a meal is dessert, often fruit.

Special foods

Jerked meat is a speciality of the Caribbean. It developed from the Carib Indian method of smoking spiced meat over fires. The meat was then cut into strips and dried in the sun. This method preserved the meat. Later, maroons (escaped slaves) used a similar method to cook wild boar in Jamaica.

Today, jerked meat is cooked at roadside stands. A charcoal fire is lit in an oil drum. The meat is placed over the fire to cook in the hot smoke. Hot chilli peppers **season** the meat and make it very spicy. It is often served with fried dumplings called festivals.

↑ Meat is smoked and sold at roadside stands.

Ingredients

sweet potato

pumpkin

mango

coconut

coconut milk

lime

ginger

banana

cinnamon

nutmeg

Many ingredients for Caribbean recipes are easy to find in supermarkets and shops.

Coconut

Coconuts grow all over the Caribbean, and are used in hundreds of different ways in Caribbean cooking. You can sometimes find fresh coconuts in shops and supermarkets. Blocks of creamed coconut and cans of coconut milk are easy to find as well. Coconut milk is made by **grating** the flesh of the coconut and mixing it with water. The **transparent** juice inside the coconut is a popular Caribbean drink, too.

Fruit

The climate of the Caribbean is ideal for growing all sorts of fruit. This book includes recipes that use some of the most common Caribbean fruits – bananas, mangoes, and limes.

plantain

Plantains

Plantains are members of the banana family. They are bigger and firmer than bananas, and need to be cooked before they can be eaten. Plantains can be hard to find outside the Caribbean, so the recipes in this book use unripe, green bananas instead.

Pumpkin

Pumpkins are grown all over the Caribbean, and are a **staple** ingredient in many dishes, both sweet and savoury. If you can't find pumpkin, you can use any sort of squash, such as butternut squash, instead.

Spices

Spices are plants or seeds with strong flavours, which are used to add taste in cooking. Caribbean cooks use a lot of spices. Some of the most common are cinnamon, nutmeg, ginger, allspice, and chilli powder. Chilli powder is very hot and spicy, so leave it out if you don't like spicy food. All of these spices can easily be bought dried, in jars or boxes.

Sweet potatoes

Sweet potatoes have orange or red skin, and orange flesh. They come from a different plant from ordinary potatoes, and are used in many Caribbean dishes.

Before you start

Which recipe should I try?

The recipes you choose to make depends on many things. Some recipes make a good main course, while others are better as starters. Some are easy, others are more difficult.

The top right-hand page of each recipe has information that can help you. It tells you how long each recipe will take and how many people it serves. You can multiply or divide the quantities if you want to cook for more or fewer people. This section also shows how difficult each dish is to make: the recipes are easy (*), medium (**), or difficult (***) to cook. The symbols in the corner can help you quickly find certain recipes. Here is a key that will help you.

 Healthy choice: These recipes are healthy to eat.

 Quick and easy: These recipes are quick and easy to make.

 Sweet treat: These recipes make a good dessert or sweet snack.

This symbol ▲ is sign of a dangerous step in a recipe. For these steps, take extra care or ask an adult to help.

Kitchen rules

There are a few basic rules you should always follow when you cook:

- Ask an adult if you can use the kitchen.
- Wash your hands before you start.
- Wear an apron to protect your clothes. Tie back long hair.
- Be very careful when using sharp knives.
- Never leave pan handles sticking out – it could be dangerous if you bump into them.
- Always wear oven gloves to lift things in and out of the oven.
- Wash fruit and vegetables before you use them.

Quantities and measurements

Ingredients for recipes can be measured in two different ways. Metric measurements use grams, litres, and millilitres. Imperial measurements use cups, ounces, and fluid ounces. In the recipes in this book you will see the following abbreviations:

tbsp = tablespoons   oz = ounces
tsp = teaspoons   ml = millilitres
g = grams   cm = centimetres

Utensils

To cook the recipes in this book, you will need these utensils, as well as kitchen essentials, such as forks, spoons, plates, and bowls.

- 2 baking tins
  (one 18cm round tin
  and one 900g loaf tin)
- chopping board
- cooling rack
- foil
- food processor or blender
- frying pan
- glass bowl
- grater
- large bowl
- large, flat, ovenproof dish
- lemon squeezer
- measuring jug
- metal or wooden skewers
- roasting tin
- rolling pin
- saucepan with lid
- set of scales
- sharp knife
- sieve or colander
- small bowl
- wooden spoon

Pumpkin soup

Pumpkin is used in both savoury and sweet dishes in the Caribbean. Although pumpkin is actually a fruit, it is usually cooked like a vegetable.

What you need

1 clove of garlic

½ onion

1kg fresh pumpkin (or 500g canned pumpkin)

1 carrot

500ml water

1 vegetable stock cube

1 tbsp sunflower oil

½ tsp chilli powder (optional)

¼ tsp dried ginger

¼ tsp cinnamon

¼ tsp allspice

400ml canned reduced-fat coconut milk

Salt and pepper

What you do

1 **Peel** the garlic and the onion, and finely **chop** them.

2 If using fresh pumpkin, carefully cut it into quarters. Lay each quarter flat on a chopping board and carefully peel it. Use a spoon to scoop out the seeds, and chop the pumpkin into bite-sized chunks.

3 Wash the carrot and chop it into pieces about the same size as the pumpkin chunks.

4 Put the water into a saucepan, and bring it to the **boil**. Crumble the stock cube into the water, and stir it until it **dissolves**. Take the stock off the heat.

5 Heat the oil in a saucepan over a medium heat. Add the chopped onion, garlic, and chilli powder (if using), and **fry** for 3 minutes.

6 Stir in the ginger, cinnamon, allspice, coconut milk, stock, and a pinch of salt and pepper.

7 Bring the soup to the boil, then **simmer** it for 5 minutes. Add the chunks of carrot and the pumpkin, and bring the soup to the boil again.

8 **Cover** the pan, and cook the soup over a low heat for 40 minutes.

9 Carefully pour the hot soup into a food processor or blender, and **blend** it on the highest setting until it is smooth.

Banana soup

In the Caribbean, this soup is usually made with another member of the banana family, plantains. Plantains need to be cooked before they can be eaten, and can be hard to find. Bananas which are not yet completely ripe, and are still slightly green, make a good substitute in this dish.

What you need

500ml water
2 unripe bananas
1 vegetable stock cube
250ml canned reduced-fat
  coconut milk
Salt and pepper
¼ tsp chilli powder
  (optional)

What you do

1 Put the water into a saucepan, and bring it to the **boil**. Crumble the stock cube into the water, and stir until it **dissolves**. Take the stock off the heat.

2 **Peel** the bananas and **slice** them into thick chunks.

3 Put the bananas, stock, coconut milk, chilli powder (if using), and a pinch of salt and pepper into a saucepan.

4 Bring the soup to the boil, then **cover** the pan and cook the soup over a low heat for 10 minutes.

5 Pour the hot soup into a food processor or blender, and **blend** it on the highest setting until it is smooth.

SATURDAY SOUPS

Soup is popular on nearly all the Caribbean islands. It is often served on Saturday mornings, to use up leftovers before cooking a big Sunday lunch the next day.

Chicken and banana skewers

For this dish, pieces of chicken and banana are threaded onto sticks called skewers, and **grilled**. As with banana soup on page 14, this dish is often made with plantains in the Caribbean. This recipe uses unripe bananas, which are still slightly green.

What you need

- 1 tbsp smooth peanut butter
- 1 tsp paprika
- ¼ tsp dried ginger
- 3 tbsp water
- 1 chicken breast
- 2 unripe bananas

What you do

1 Put the peanut butter, paprika, and ginger in a saucepan, and add the water. Heat gently over a low heat until the peanut butter has melted into the other ingredients. Pour the sauce into a bowl.

2 Cut the chicken into small pieces. Put the chicken pieces into the bowl with the sauce, and mix well so the chicken is coated with the sauce. Leave it to **marinate** in the sauce for 1 hour.

3 **Peel** the bananas and **slice** them into thick chunks.

Ready to eat: 1 hour 30 minutes (including 1 hour to marinate the chicken). Difficulty: *. Serves 2.

4 Take the chicken pieces out of the sauce. Push a piece of chicken, then a piece of banana on to a skewer until it is full. Then make three more.

5 Brush the skewered chicken and banana with the left-over sauce.

6 Grill the skewered chicken and banana under a medium grill for 5 minutes, until they are golden brown on one side. Turn them and grill them on the other side for 5 minutes.

VEGETARIAN VARIATION

Try making vegetarian skewers by replacing the chicken with pieces of pumpkin or sweet potato. Cut the vegetables into pieces, and boil them in water for 10 minutes before marinating them in the same way as the chicken.

Chicken in coconut sauce

Coconuts grow on most Caribbean islands, and are used in many dishes. Both their flesh and their milk are very **nutritious**. In this dish, coconut milk makes a creamy sauce for the chicken.

What you need

2 chicken breasts
1 clove of garlic
½ onion
2 spring onions
1 tbsp sunflower oil
¼ tsp chilli powder
   (optional)
¼ tsp curry powder
½ tsp dried thyme
300ml canned
   reduced-fat
   coconut milk

What you do

1 **Chop** the chicken breasts into small pieces.

2 **Peel** the skin from the garlic clove and onion, and finely chop them.

3 Cut the tops and bottoms off the spring onions, and finely chop them.

4 Heat the oil in a saucepan. Add the chicken pieces, chopped garlic, onion, chilli powder (if using), and curry powder.

5 **Fry** the mixture for 10 minutes, stirring occasionally.

6 Add the chopped spring onions, thyme, and coconut milk to the saucepan.

7 Bring the mixture to the **boil**, then reduce the heat and **simmer** for about 40 minutes, until the sauce has thickened.

8 Serve with plain boiled rice.

seafood bake

The sea around the Caribbean islands provides the people with lots of fish. This recipe makes enough to feed four people, served with boiled rice. You can use fresh or frozen fish – if using frozen, make sure you move it from the freezer to the fridge about 12 hours before you start cooking, so it is completely **thawed**.

What you need

2 cloves of garlic
2 onions
1 aubergine
4 medium potatoes
150g cabbage
240g pumpkin
30g fresh parsley
4 fish fillets
100ml olive oil
½ tsp chilli powder (optional)
240g peeled prawns

What you do

1. **Preheat** the oven to 190°C/375°F/gas mark 5.

2. **Peel** the the garlic and onions, and finely **chop** them.

3. Chop the aubergine into pieces about 1cm across.

4. Peel or scrub the potatoes, and **slice** them thinly.

5. Finely **shred** the cabbage.

6. Peel the skin from the pumpkin, remove the seeds, and cut it into pieces about 1cm across.

7. Finely chop the parsley.

8. Put the fish into a saucepan. Cover it with water, bring to the **boil**, and then **simmer** for about 5 minutes.

9. **Drain** the fish. **Flake** it into a bowl, removing any skin and bones.

10 Heat half the olive oil in a saucepan over a low heat. Add the chopped onion, garlic, aubergine, and chilli powder (if using). **Fry** for 10 minutes, until the aubergine is soft.

11 Add the flaked fish to the onion and aubergine mixture, and mix together well.

12 In this order, spoon a layer of each ingredient into an ovenproof dish:
- potato slices
- fish mixture
- shredded cabbage
- prawns
- chopped pumpkin
- parsley

13 **Drizzle** the rest of the oil over the top of the dish. **Cover** it with foil, and **bake** for 30 minutes.

14 Remove the foil, and bake for a further 20 minutes.

21

Baked fish with lime and orange juice

You can use all sorts of different fish in this recipe. It is often cooked with red snapper in the Caribbean, but if you can't get hold of any, try using tilapia or Pacific cod. If you use frozen fish, move it from the freezer to the fridge about 12 hours before you start cooking so it is completely **thawed**.

What you need

2 cloves of garlic
½ onion
2 spring onions
2 limes
1 orange
2 fish fillets
½ tsp sugar
½ tsp dried thyme
¼ tsp chilli powder
   (optional)
Salt and pepper

What you do

1 **Preheat** the oven to 200°C/ 400°F/gas mark 6.

2 **Peel** the garlic cloves and onion and finely **chop** them.

3 Cut the tops and bottoms off the spring onions and discard them. Finely chop the spring onions.

4 Cut the limes and orange in half. Squeeze the juice out of them with a lemon squeezer.

5 Put the fish fillets into an ovenproof dish. Pour 200ml water around them.

6 Pour the lime and orange juice over the fish.

7 Put the chopped garlic, sugar, thyme, onion, spring onions, chilli powder (if using), and a pinch of salt and pepper on to the fish.

8 **Cover** the dish with foil, and **bake** the fish for 30 minutes. Serve it with plain boiled rice.

RED SNAPPER

Red snapper is one of the most popular fish in the Caribbean. It is the most common species of snapper, but other species come in all sorts of different colours and patterns, including stripy snapper!

Fish with rice and peas

Different kinds of firm white fish can be used to cook this dish. Tilapia is fished all year round in the Caribbean and has a mild taste. Red snapper has a firm texture and a slightly sweet, nutty flavour. In the Caribbean, fish is often **grilled** in a wet banana leaf. Caribbean dishes called "peas" actually have beans rather than peas in them.

What you need

2 fish fillets
1 small red onion
¼ green pepper
¼ red pepper
1 clove of garlic
½ tsp paprika
2 tsp butter
150g rice
150g canned red
    kidney beans
1 spring onion
Salt and pepper

What you do

1 **Preheat** the oven to 190°C/375°F/ gas mark 5.

2 **Slice** the red onion into rings, cut the green and red pepper into slices, and crush the garlic.

3 Place each fillet on a sheet of foil. Slice the fish open and stuff each one with half the red onion, garlic, paprika, slices of pepper, and butter.

4 Wrap the foil over the fish and **bake** them in the oven for 20–30 minutes.

5 While the fish is cooking, cook the rice according to the instructions on the packet.

6 Add the kidney beans to the rice and continue to cook for another 2 minutes.

7 Cut the tops and bottoms off the spring onion and discard them. **Chop** the spring onion and mix it into the rice.

8 **Season** the rice with salt and pepper and serve with the fish.

Banana curry

As with banana soup (page 14), and chicken and banana skewers (page 16), this dish is usually made with plantains in the Caribbean. If you can find them, cook them in the same way as the bananas in this recipe. If you can't, use unripe bananas, which are still slightly green, instead. Serve your curry with plain, boiled rice.

What you need

15g butter or margarine

15g cornflour

1 tsp curry powder

400ml canned reduced-fat coconut milk

¼ tsp nutmeg

2 unripe bananas

Salt and pepper

1 **Preheat** the oven to 230°C/ 450°F/gas mark 8.

2 Melt the butter or margarine in a saucepan over a low heat. When it is melted, take the saucepan off the heat, and gradually add the cornflour, stirring all the time, to make a thick paste.

3 Still keeping the pan off the heat, gradually stir the coconut milk into the paste. Do this very slowly so you don't get lumps in the sauce.

4 Put the sauce back on to the heat, and heat gradually, stirring all the time, until it becomes thick and starts to bubble.

5 Add the nutmeg, curry powder, and a pinch of salt and pepper to the sauce, and stir.

6 **Peel** the bananas and **slice** them into thick pieces. Arrange them in the bottom of an ovenproof dish.

Ready to eat: 50 minutes. Difficulty: **. Serves 2.

 7 Pour the sauce over the bananas.

8 **Bake** your curry in the oven, uncovered, for 30 minutes.

PLANTAIN CRISPS
Plantains can be fried, boiled, or baked. Plantain crisps (a bit like potato crisps) are made by cutting plantains into thin slices, then deep-frying them and sprinkling them with salt.

Bean and egg salad

Caribbean cooks use many types of beans. Beans are filling and **nutritious**. This salad contains three different types – kidney beans, haricot beans, and green beans. You could eat this salad as a main course, perhaps with some crusty bread.

What you need

- 1 red onion
- 2 tbsp olive oil
- 1 tbsp balsamic vinegar or red wine vinegar
- 1 tbsp mayonnaise
- 200g canned kidney beans
- 200g canned haricot beans
- 300g green beans
- 2 or 3 large lettuce leaves
- 2 eggs

What you do

1. **Peel** the skin from the onion and finely **chop** it.

2. In a bowl, mix together the oil, vinegar, and mayonnaise.

3. **Drain** the kidney beans and haricot beans. Add them to the bowl, together with the onion.

4. Cut the ends off the green beans. If they are long, cut them in half.

5. Bring a saucepan of water to the **boil**, and add the green beans to the pan. Boil them for 5 minutes, then drain the water from the beans and leave them to **cool**.

6. Carefully place the eggs in a saucepan. Add enough water to cover them. Bring the water to the boil, then reduce the heat and **simmer** the eggs for 8 minutes.

7. Use a spoon to lift the eggs out of the water. Hold them under cold running water to cool them, then peel off the shells.

8 Put the lettuce leaves on a plate. Put the kidney and haricot bean mixture in the middle of the lettuce leaves.

9 Arrange the green beans in a circle around the bean mixture. **Slice** the eggs and arrange the slices in a circle around the green beans.

Green, red, and yellow salad

This colourful and refreshing salad is ideal for a hot day. It could be served as a side dish, or you could eat it with crusty bread as a snack or light lunch.

What you need

- 1 green pepper
- 1 yellow pepper
- 1 red pepper
- 2 large tomatoes
- ½ lettuce (for example, iceberg or cos)
- 1 lime
- 3 tbsp olive oil
- ½ tbsp white wine vinegar
- ¼ tsp paprika
- ¼ tsp sugar
- Salt and pepper

What you do

1 Cut the tops off the peppers, and scoop out the seeds. Cut the peppers into round **slices**.

2 Cut the tomatoes into thin slices.

3 **Shred** the lettuce.

4 Arrange the salad in a bowl in layers. Put a layer of green peppers at the bottom, followed by a layer of tomatoes, a layer of yellow peppers, and a layer of red peppers.

5 Top the salad with the shredded lettuce.

6 Cut the lime in half. Using a lemon squeezer, squeeze the juice out of one half of it.

7 Put the lime juice, olive oil, vinegar, paprika, sugar, and a pinch of salt and pepper into a small bowl, and mix them together well to make a dressing for the salad.

8 **Drizzle** the dressing evenly over the salad. Try not to mix it in, or you will spoil the layers you have built up.

SERVING THE SALAD
If you can, make this salad in a glass bowl, so you can see the different layers through the side of the bowl. When you serve it, use a knife to cut it into colourful wedges.

Sweet potato and pumpkin pudding

Sweet potatoes and pumpkins are used in both savoury and sweet Caribbean dishes. This dessert combines sweet potato and pumpkin with spices and dried fruit.

What you need

200g sweet potatoes
200g pumpkin
1 tsp dried ginger
½ tsp nutmeg
½ tsp cinnamon
½ tsp vanilla essence
50g raisins
10g butter or
 margarine
100ml canned
 coconut milk
50g brown sugar

What you do

1 **Preheat** the oven to 200°C/ 400°F/gas mark 6.

2 **Peel** the sweet potatoes and the pumpkin. **Grate** both of them into a bowl.

3 Add the ginger, nutmeg, cinnamon, vanilla essence, and raisins to the bowl of grated sweet potatoes and pumpkin.

4 Melt the butter or margarine in a saucepan.

5 In a bowl, mix together the coconut milk, sugar, and melted butter or margarine. Pour this mixture into the sweet potato and pumpkin mixture, and stir everything together.

6 Using your fingers, rub some extra butter or margarine into an 18cm round baking tin.

7 Spoon the pudding mixture into the baking tin. **Bake** it in the oven for 1½ hours.

8 Take the pudding out of the oven, and let it stand for 10 minutes before serving.

Banana bread

Banana bread is cooked all over the Caribbean. You could eat it as a pudding with cream or as a snack. It is best to use very ripe bananas.

What you need

100g butter or margarine
250g brown sugar
1 egg
3 ripe bananas
350g self-raising flour
½ tsp cinnamon
½ tsp nutmeg
100ml milk
1 tsp vanilla essence

What you do

1 **Preheat** the oven to 180°C/350°F/gas mark 4.

2 **Peel** the bananas, and, using a fork, **mash** them in a bowl.

3 Using a wooden spoon, **beat** the butter and sugar together in a bowl. Add the egg, and beat the mixture for 1 minute.

4 Add the mashed bananas to the butter, sugar, and egg mixture, and mix everything together.

5 Using a metal spoon, **fold** the flour, cinnamon, and nutmeg into the mixture.

6 Add the milk and vanilla essence to the mixture. Stir the mixture well.

7 Using your fingers, rub some butter or margarine into a 900g loaf tin.

8 Spoon the banana bread mixture into the loaf tin. **Bake** it in the oven for 1 hour.

9 Using an oven glove, tip it out onto a cooling rack to **cool** before you **slice** it.

IS IT COOKED?

You can check whether the banana bread is cooked by sticking a skewer or a sharp knife straight down into the middle of the bread. If the skewer comes out clean, the bread is ready. If it comes out with some mixture stuck to it, put the bread back in the oven for a few more minutes.

Pancakes with mangoes

You need a really ripe mango for this dish. Check if it is ripe by squeezing it gently – if you feel it "give", it is ripe.

What you need

1 ripe mango
1 tbsp caster sugar
1 egg
175ml milk
80g plain flour
½ tsp nutmeg
2 tbsp sunflower oil

What you do

1 **Peel** the skin from the mango. Cut the flesh from either side of the flat stone.

2 Put the mango flesh into a food processor or blender with the caster sugar. **Blend** the mango on the highest setting until it becomes a **pulp**.

3 Spoon the mango pulp into a bowl, then clean the blender.

4 Put the egg and milk into the blender and turn it to its highest setting for about 30 seconds.

5 Turn the blender to low, and gradually pour in the flour, then add the nutmeg. Blend the batter until it is smooth.

6 Put the batter into the fridge, and leave it to stand for 30 minutes.

7 Heat ½ tbsp oil in a medium-sized non-stick frying pan over a medium heat. Put 3 tbsp of the pancake batter into the pan, and swirl it around so that the batter spreads out.

8 Cook the pancake for about 1 minute, then turn it over and cook the other side for the same time.

9 Slide the pancake out of the pan onto a plate, and repeat steps 7 and 8 until you have made four pancakes.

10 Divide the mango pulp between the four pancakes, spreading it over half of the pancake.

11 Fold the other half of the pancake over the top of the filling, and fold the pancake again.

Mango ice cream

It can get very hot in the Caribbean, so ice cream is popular. To make this recipe, you need really ripe mangoes – see page 36 for how to check whether a mango is ripe.

What you need

2 ripe mangoes
300ml milk
4 egg yolks
100g caster sugar
300ml double cream

What you do

1 **Peel** the skin from the mangoes. Cut the flesh from the stone, and put the flesh into a food processor or blender. **Blend** the mango on the highest setting until it becomes a **pulp**.

2 Put the milk into a saucepan. Heat it until it is hot, but not **boiling**.

3 To separate the egg yolks from the whites, carefully crack the egg. Keeping the yolk in one half of the shell, let the white drip into a bowl. Pass the yolk from one half of the shell to the other until all the white has dripped out. Put the yolk in a separate bowl. Do this for all four eggs. **Beat** the egg yolks and sugar together in a bowl until they are well mixed.

4 Gradually stir the hot milk into the egg and sugar mixture, stirring all the time.

5 Pour the mixture back into the saucepan. Cook it over a low heat until it thickens (this should take about 10 minutes).

Ready to eat: 5 hours 30 minutes (including 5 hours to freeze). Difficulty: **.
Serves 4.

6 Pour the mixture into a bowl, then **whisk** in the cream and the pulped mango.

7 Put the mixture into the freezer. After an hour, take the bowl out of the freezer, and **mash** the mixture with a fork to break up any lumps.

8 Repeat step 7 until the ice cream is set. This should take about 4 or 5 hours, depending on how cold your freezer is.

Ginger beer

Ginger beer is drunk all over the Caribbean. It is often sold on street stalls. Each stall has a huge block of ice, and the ginger beer seller chips some ice off the block, puts it into a cup, then pours the ginger beer over the top to make a wonderfully cool and refreshing drink.

Although ginger beer is quick and easy to make, you have to leave it to stand for a couple of days so that the taste of the ginger spreads through the whole drink.

What you need

A large piece of fresh
   ginger (about 30g)
1½ litres water
175g caster sugar

What you do

1 **Peel** the skin from the ginger, then **grate** the ginger finely. Keep your fingers clear!

2 Put the water into a large saucepan and bring it to the **boil**.

3 Add the grated ginger and caster sugar to the boiling water. Stir everything together, then turn off the heat.

4 Put a lid on the pan, and leave it to stand somewhere cool for a couple of days.

6 Pour the ginger beer through a sieve into a jug, then pour it into a plastic or glass bottle.

5 Keep the bottle in the fridge until you want to drink the ginger beer.

GINGER MEDICINE
Ginger is used by many people as a medicine.
In the Caribbean, a hot drink made from ginger is
used to relieve stomach pains and flu.

Coconut milkshake

Coconuts are used in many ways in Caribbean life. The flesh of the coconut is an ingredient in lots of different dishes. The liquid in the middle of the coconut is a popular drink. The coconut shell is turned into utensils such as spoons and cups, and the leaves of the coconut tree are used to make roofs for houses.

This coconut milkshake is refreshing and easy to make.

What you need

200ml vanilla ice
  cream
200ml canned
  coconut milk
100ml milk
½ tsp nutmeg

What you do

1. Put all the ingredients into a food processor or blender.

2. **Blend** the milkshake on the highest setting until it is smooth.

3. Pour the milkshake into two glasses. That's it!

OTHER MILKSHAKES

You can make milkshakes in all sorts of different flavours. Try replacing the coconut milk with mashed bananas or strawberries, or with cold, sweet cocoa.

ADDING ICE

To make your milkshakes even more refreshing on a hot day, put ice cubes in the bottom of the glasses before pouring in the milkshake.

Further information

Here are some places to find out more about the Caribbean and its cooking.

Books

Cooking the Caribbean Way by Cheryl Davidson Kaufman (Lerner, 2009)
Food in the Caribbean by Polly Goodman (PowerKids Press, 2008)
Foods of the Caribbean by Barbara Sheen (KidHaven Press, 2007)
The Second International Cookbook for Kids by Matthew Locricchio (Marshall
  Cavendish, 2008)

Websites

www.globalgourmet.com/destinations/caribbean

www.dishbase.com/recipes/caribbean

www.ichef.com/clubs/39

Healthy eating

This diagram shows the types and proportion of food you should eat to stay healthy. Eat plenty of foods from the *bread, rice, potatoes, pasta* group and plenty from the *fruit and vegetables* group. Eat some foods from the *milk and dairy* group and the *meat, fish, eggs, beans* group. Foods from the smallest group are not necessary for a healthy diet so eat these in small amounts or only occasionally.

Healthy eating, Caribbean style

Caribbean cooking uses many ingredients from the *bread, rice, potatoes, pasta* group – for example, people often eat rice as part of their main meal. The rest of the meal might consist of chicken, fish, or beans, along with vegetables such as pumpkin, plaintains, or peppers. Coconut is used in sauces and desserts, so you can see how healthy caribbean cooking is!

↑ The Eatwell food plate shows the proportion of food from each food group you should eat to achieve a healthy, balanced diet. This takes account of everything you eat, including snacks.

Glossary

bake cook something in the oven

beat mix something together strongly using a fork, spoon, or whisk

blend mix ingredients together in a blender or food processor

boil cook a liquid on the hob. Boiling liquid bubbles and steams strongly.

chop cut something into pieces using a knife

cool allow hot food to become cold. You should always allow food to cool before putting it in the fridge.

cover put a lid on a pan, or foil over a dish

deep-fried cooked in deep, hot oil

dissolve mix something into a liquid until it disappears

drain remove liquid, usually by pouring something into a colander or sieve

drizzle pour something very slowly and evenly

flake break something, for example a piece of fish, into small pieces

fold mix ingredients together very slowly and carefully

fry cook something in oil in a pan

grate break something, such as cheese, into small pieces using a grater

grill cook something under the grill

marinate soak something, such as meat or fish, in a mixture called a marinade before cooking, so that it absorbs the taste of the mixture

mash crush something, for example potato, until it is soft and pulpy

nutritious good, healthy food to eat

peel remove the skin of a fruit or vegetable

preheat turn on the oven or grill in advance, so that it is hot when you are ready to use it

pulp mixture that has been mashed or blended until smooth

season give extra flavour to food by adding salt or pepper

shred cut or tear something, for example a lettuce, into small pieces

simmer cook a liquid on the hob. Simmering liquid bubbles and steams gently.

slice cut something into thin, flat pieces

staple a main ingredient, one found in many dishes

thaw defrost something which has been frozen

transparent see-through

whisk mix ingredients using a whisk

Index